P. C. McAndrew

12-7
12-20
233

# THE SECRET OF COOKING FOR CATS

Other Books by Martin A. Gardner & Clare Barnes, Jr.

THE SECRET OF COOKING FOR DOGS

MARTIN A. GARDNER

# The Secret of
# Cooking for Cats

Illustrations by Clare Barnes, Jr.

DOUBLEDAY & COMPANY, INC.
GARDEN CITY, NEW YORK
1965

LIBRARY OF CONGRESS CATALOG CARD NUMBER 65–19928
COPYRIGHT © 1965 BY MARTIN A. GARDNER AND CLARE BARNES, JR.
PRINTED IN THE UNITED STATES OF AMERICA
FIRST EDITION

## ACKNOWLEDGMENTS

I am deeply indebted to a number of people who helped a great deal in the preparation of this book.

I am happy to express deepest gratitude to Dr. James R. Kinney, who has been practicing for many years, over thirty of them, at Ellin Prince Speyer Hospital in New York City where he was chief veterinarian and director. Dr. Kinney gave generously of time, effort, knowledge, and professional advice, and his suggestions were most helpful.

Many thanks to Miss Clementine Paddleford, Food Editor of the New York *Herald Tribune* and Food Editor of *This Week Magazine*, whose kind help was of great value in the preparation of some of the recipes in this book.

The public relations departments of the various commercial pet food companies deserve thanks for generously providing me with pamphlets and other printed materials that were full of valuable information.

Finally, my appreciation to the many anonymous cat owners who contributed much information and help in preparing the recipes in this book.

*New York City*                                        Martin A. Gardner
*April 1965*

# CONTENTS

# THE SECRET OF COOKING FOR CATS

*Cats are complex characters.*

Attention Fellow Cat Lovers . . .

One of the greatest areas of discussion about cats is proper feeding. Many people feel that feeding a cat is simple: just a kind word, a pleasant smile, and a hearty bowl of milk. This is a mistake. Although feeding a cat is not as simple as the solitary bowl-of-milk method, it is not difficult either. (By the way, some veterinarians feel that the bowl-of-milk-a-day diet can be quite dangerous for adult cats, particularly altered males, since milk is high in calcium and can lead to the formation of kidney stones!) Your own veterinarian will be glad to give you his opinion on this. It just takes a little common sense.

You see, cats are complex characters. They're not the simple, straightforward animals that dogs are. They have whims. They have prejudices. They have sensitivity. And, this carries over into their eating habits. There may be days and days when your cat won't touch a morsel of food, even if it's prepared with all the loving care that only a true cat lover like you can give. This refusal of food may not even be an indication that your pet is ill. He may have just tired of his daily fare.

That's the point of this cookbook. The cat's appetite must be encouraged by variety, and not suppressed by the monotony of the same meal with the same appearance in the same bowl at every sitting. Variety at mealtime is a key factor in cultivating a calm, collected cat.

In the search for variety for your favorite feline, you will probably come across foods that your cat despises with the kind of venom he usually reserves for dogs. This is natural. There are ways, though, to compensate for your cat's prima donna attitude, especially if his nose is turned up at necessary and essential foods. This is one of the secrets of cooking for cats: how to nourish without alienating!

You will also find that there are some foods which you should not prepare for your pet cat! Therefore, you must learn the secret of how *not* to cook for your cat, too!

Included in this book are recipes and information using all the

*You will probably come across food that your cat despises.*

different types of food your cat ought to like and are best for him.
Meat, fish, milk, soup, vegetables, and chicken are just some of the
various types of food that will make your pet a cute, capricious kitty.

The recipes are geared for the average house cat. How much and
how often do you feed him? You may have to adjust the amounts of
food to compensate for your own pet's appetite. Usually, you should
feed him enough so that he isn't ravenous at his next meal. Perhaps
you'll want to check with your veterinarian about the amount to feed
your cat. This is important. You see, you could feed him too much.
(Cats have a tendency to overeat!) Remember: you should never
feed your cat so much that he can't eat his next meal! For the average cat, from birth to weaning, feed him four times a day; from
weaning to five months, three times a day; from five months to eight
months, twice a day; and after eight months, just once a day.

Now, there's more to cooking for cats than just standing over an

*If you make his main meal interesting, diverse, and full of adventure*
*and romance, he'll love you madly.*

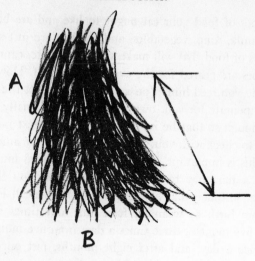

*Detailed sketch of angora cat's paw*

unlimited range. For example, did you know that cats who tend to get fat can go on a reducing diet? (If your pet is *too* fat, his life may be shortened, just like a human who is overweight.) By the same token, a cat who is too thin can go on a gaining diet. By asking your veterinarian, you can find out which diet to follow to remedy having a fat cat.

Your veterinarian is the best authority on the proper care and feeding of your cat. The veterinarian is a completely trained doctor who is dedicated to animals. So take your cat to the veterinarian for regular check-ups as well as for an emergency! *Don't be afraid to consult your veterinarian at any time.* He's primarily concerned with your cat's health, just as your own doctor is concerned with your health.

A final word: there is no reason why you *must* cook for your pet. If he likes commercial pet food at every meal, give it to him. The commercial pet food is good, generally. The commercial pet food manufacturers spend thousands of dollars in research every year so that their products will appeal to your cat and his well-being.

But if your cat would prefer you to cook for him, either on a regular basis or just to augment commercially prepared foods, this book

## Use of tail to communicate

Leftovers again!

That happens to be my bowl, Rover!

A plethora of catnip

What's for dessert?

Quick studies of cat's whiskers

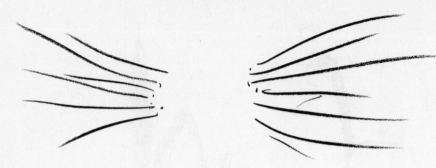

Front view looking head-on

Side view

Rear view of whiskers somewhat hidden by back of cat's head

is for you. Of course, the information and recipes that follow are intended to serve only as a guide. They are not the final word on meal-making for your pet.

For house cats, meals are the most important event of the day. So here's a chance to win your cat's undying love (if you don't have it already). If you make his main meal interesting, diverse, and full of adventure and romance, he'll love you madly. With this in mind, dear cat lover, we hope you enjoy this cookbook for cats, and that you find that it answers some of the questions you may have about feeding your pet. Happy cooking!

# 1

# Meat Me for Dinner, Baby

*Most cats agree it really doesn't matter whether meat is raw or cooked.*

Well, it's dinner time for your cat again! And you know very well that that old rascal needs meat! Whether he's a lean, lanky bookshelf type or a fat, complacent maharajah, it's the most important food he can get for promoting growth and energy. Of course, it will be no surprise to any of you expert pet owners if your cat jumps up on your lap some evening and purrs seductively in your ear, "Meat me for dinner, baby." So, fellow cat lovers, let's get right to the meat of the problem.

Even though there's no arguing that meat is *the* basic food for cats, there's been a Great Debate among cat owners whether or not raw or cooked meat is better. The Raw School says that raw lean beef makes the best meal in town. Especially for breeding cats. (Now who could possibly need *more* energy than a male cat who gets a sexy summons from his girl friend for a nightly command performance?) On the other hand, the Cooked School contends that cooked meat is preferable because it is more digestible.

Most cats agree that it really doesn't matter whether their meat is raw or cooked. Actually, the only food that *must* be cooked for cats is fish (see "Just for the Halibut!"). So there's no need to be concerned about the Great Debate over raw vs. cooked meat. Just ask your cat for his opinion. After all, it *is* his stomach! He's bound to prefer one or the other—or both!

When you buy ground beef for your cat, you should be especially careful. Some cat owners feel that ready-ground beef is too fat. Or not fresh. Or not *all* beef. Now no one is accusing your butcher of cheating you, but he may not know that cats need all beef in their beef. He may think he's doing you a service by including other things (sawdust, orange peels, toilet tissue) in his ground beef for your cat, with an eye to adding roughage. But that's your job, not his. After all, you know what's best for your cat. If your pet doesn't like sawdust—he just doesn't like sawdust! There's no getting around it. So make sure that, when you get ground beef for your cat, it's all beef. And lean. Be certain that all the fat has been cut away *before* grinding. The reason? Usually ground beef prepared especially for cats is fattier than ground beef prepared especially for humans. Thus, any *extra* fat will make the fat content too high for your cat. Also, watch that the meat is ground at least twice. Obviously this *fattier* meat is going to be harder to chew. And the harder it is to chew, the more it should be ground. Of course, if you're lucky enough to own your own meat grinder, you can grind it yourself before serving. The point is: ground beef must be *ground!*

Say, do you have a loose cat? One who heads for secluded corners at the slightest suggestion? Well, if your cat has a diarrhea problem you don't need to add a supplement to his meat. Otherwise you do. Remember: cats can't live by meat alone! If they are fed meat without a supplement, their health begins to deteriorate. As a matter of

*No one is accusing your butcher of cheating you. . . .*

fact, there's even a strong possibility that, fed exclusively over a long period of time, a straight meat diet can kill your pet, since it obviously can *un*balance his diet! Make sure you avoid any possible ill health and include a supplement in his meat. Actually this would be true if you fed your cat an exclusive diet of any one thing; for example even chicken fricassee day after day could be harmful. The important thing to remember is variety.

Supplements take many forms, but it is generally accepted that for your kittens you should add baby food, and as they grow older, add wheat-germ cereal or shredded wheat, or any of the non-starchy cooked vegetables (see "Rough Rough").

How much do you add? Usually one or two teaspoons per serving, depending on his size and age. But not too much! If you give your cat or kitten too much starchy food, he's going to lose some of the muscle firmness and stamina that make him the neighborhood acrobat. If you mash the wheat germ or shredded wheat into the meat, the meat will soften and moisten it. Remember: supplements should not be too rough or too dry.

Maybe you don't know what's the best kind of meat for your cat. Or, if you're one of those don't-get-*me*-near-a-stove types, you may not even know what's the best kind of people food! Well, it is doubtful that you fall into both of these categories. But, just in case

*Your cat may turn up his nose at horsemeat.*

you have some questions, beef is the best meat for your cat (and for you, too). But usually the cost of beef makes it off limits for cats. That is, if you buy beef especially for your pet. Naturally, there's no problem if you use some of the shards of beef that would ordinarily become waste scraps when preparing your own dinner, or if you use leftovers. The one exception to the rule is kittens. Many cat owners will go to the expense of buying lean beef just for their kittens for a short while during the time when they're learning to eat meat. Some people serve lean beef only when it's to be eaten raw, and use horsemeat when they intend to cook. On the whole, horsemeat spoils more quickly than does beef. Of course, with modern refrigeration, there's little to fear. If your cat turns up his nose at horsemeat, then serve him another kind of meat.

Here are some of the other kinds of meat for cats: chicken is a big favorite. But be careful your cat doesn't become too enamored of it and start to refuse other things. If your cat is recuperating from some illness, it is usually recommended that he have some chicken. The thing to remember is that, like fish, chicken must be boned.

Lamb is high in protein, like horsemeat, but it is too fat. Pork is usually not served to cats. It's too fat and, by the time you trim off the fat, too expensive.

Liver, heart, and kidney are other cat favorites. Liver can either be

*Well, it's dinnertime for your cat again!*

beef or chicken. Beef liver is a particular favorite, except that it tends to be too laxative. If you're going to serve kidney regularly, make sure it is beef. Beef heart and kidney are inexpensive and they add variety, too.

If your pet happens to be one of those optimistic Wall Street cats, then feed him bull meat. Where do you find such a delicacy? Well, someday, take a plunge into the market and ask your butcher. Some butchers keep a supply of it especially for pets. Ground up like beef it is excellent and not too fat. If you serve bull meat once in a while, your cat will love you even more, and no doubt your stock with him will go up!

Here are a few things to remember when you prepare meat for your cat. You can cook meat after it's been ground without fear of having it stick together, making hamburgers. Cook meat in a double boiler over a low flame with little or no water. Stir and mash it while it is cooking. It takes only two or three minutes, since the less it is cooked the more tender it is. You may want to use a pressure cooker, or cook the meat in the oven to make sure that the natural juices stay in the meat. This way no nutrition is lost. If you decide to give your cat meat that is not ground, make sure you cut it up into small pieces before serving it. Cats may have big stomachs, but they have small mouths!

So when dinner rolls around again, friends, try a little variety in your cat's meat course. You don't have to be first chef at the Waldorf to prepare meat for your pet. It's really quite simple!

## WHEATBURGER WHOMP

*2 tablespoons raw ground beef*
*½ shredded wheat biscuit*
*¼ cup milk*

Mash raw beef into flat patty. Shred biscuit on top. Fold patty over so that biscuit is concealed. Place in bowl, add milk, and serve.

## LIVER AND ONION SPECIAL

> 2 *tablespoons beef liver*
> ½ *small onion*
> *Margarine*
> 1 *tablespoon cottage cheese*

Cut liver and onion into small pieces. Sauté for 1 minute in margarine. Mix with cottage cheese. Serve.

## MEAT LOAF MANGLE

> 2 *tablespoons leftover meat loaf*
> 1 *tablespoon sour cream*
> *Salt*

Warm meat loaf. Mash. Mix with sour cream. Add some salt. Serve.

## CAPTAIN KIDNEY SPECIAL

> 4 *tablespoons raw beef kidney*
> 1 *tablespoon strained baby vegetables*

Cut raw kidney into bite-sized chunks. Warm vegetables. Combine with meat in cat bowl. Serve.

## MEAT STEW

> 1 *small onion*
> ½ *green pepper*
> *Margarine*
> ¼ *pound ground beef*

Dice onion and pepper. Sauté in margarine. Add some ground beef. Cook until brown, about 5 minutes, adding water if necessary to keep moist. Serve warm.

## LAMB KIDNEY SPECIAL*

1 egg
Lamb kidney
1 small onion
Margarine

Boil egg 4 minutes. Cut up about 2 tablespoons lamb kidney into small chunks. Dice onion. Sauté onion in margarine and add kidney. Sauté about 1 minute or until lightly browned. Mix with egg and serve.

## QUICK LUNCH

3 tablespoons leftover meat loaf
2 teaspoons strained vegetable baby food

Mix and mash meat loaf and baby food. Warm in saucepan for 1 minute. Serve.

## MEAT A LA PETROZINI*

¼ pound chopped meat
1 carrot
1 onion
Margarine
1 small can tomato sauce
Grated cheese

Mash meat and place in skillet. Dice carrot and onion. Cook in margarine until meat is brown, stirring and turning continually. Cover with tomato sauce, continue cooking for 1 minute. Place in bowl and top with grated cheese

*Recipes marked with an asterisk (*) throughout are rewards and special treats (see Chapter 11).

## TEXAS STEAKS*

> *1 small onion*
> *1 small piece of steak (cut from your own dinner)*

Dice onion and place on top of steak. Broil steak until brown on outside, rare inside (just a few minutes). Cut into small pieces. Place in bowl. Include any natural gravy or blood from steak. Serve.


## INSTANT DINNER

> *Leftover veal*
> *Dry cat food*
> *Milk*

Cut up some leftover veal into small chunks. Mix with dry cat food and some milk. Serve.

# 2
# All Souped Up

*Give him an elegant meal of soup.*

Just before your cat starts to get ready for an evening at the theater, make sure he's in the right mood. And perhaps the best way to do this is to give him an elegant meal of soup. This will elevate his spirits more than any champagne.

No matter how you look at it, soup is the answer. You see, the main appeal of soup for cats is purely theatrical. It provides Variety! And as you know, your cat needs variety in his meals. Naturally this doesn't always mean a change in the type of food he gets, but it can mean a change in the way it's prepared to make it interesting and appealing to any cat—even the sad-faced Buster Keaton types.

Variety is important. Why? Because it whets the appetite. You know yourself that if you have the same meal prepared in the same way each time, you soon lose your appetite for it. But if the manner of preparation varies, not only do you look forward to the meal, but your appetite is increased. Another important point is that variety in meals can bluff the body into performing differently. If your cat

*Soup is the answer.*

*There are some foods he just won't touch.*

finds himself regularly *not regular*, a change in meal, for example, soup, can start him off being regularly regular again. Try it! This may be purely psychosomatic, but it seems to be the kind of theatrical tour de force that works on cats.

Your cat may not be the type who is easily bluffed, but a little psychological camouflage will probably work on him. And soup is just the camouflage you need. Let's face it, there are some foods, like certain green, leafy vegetables, that he just won't touch. The answer? Camouflage them in a bit of soup. He'll be tricked into getting these much-needed vegetables more easily than you thought possible. The trick is to mash them well so he won't pick out the "objectionable" vegetables as he slurps down a bowlful of succulent stew.

If your pet is a meat-and-potato man, or strictly dry-food, and he doesn't drink much, he needs some additional fluid. Well, start ringing the bell in the soup kitchen! Yes, soup will help give him the fluids he needs. After all, the fluid balance in his system must be maintained, just as the fluid balance in a human's system must be maintained. This is why a dish of fresh water must be kept near his food bowl. Usually your cat will drink some water each day, since his body requires fluid. If he's not a drinker of any great proportions, or you want to make sure he does have some additional fluid intake, then you can be *sure* if he gets a little soup occasionally. The value of fluid in his system is that it keeps him on his toes: that is, well-balanced. Although cats do perspire a little, most of their elimination of waste is by defecation and urination. And, without liquids, he'd have quite a struggle.

Here's more food for thought! When you make soup for your cat, make it a little stewy rather than a clear broth. Although cats lick and slurp their food, too much broth will tend to have a laxative effect on them. Soup should be a *bit* liquid rather than thin and clear, for the most part. Another important thing to remember is that soup should be warm, not hot. Just like human baby food. If you are perplexed about the quantity of soup to feed your cat, remember that he should get no more soup than he would any other kind of food. Just a few ounces is about par for the soup course. If you have an old cat, soup is the perfect fireside feast. Our older citizens seem to need food which will retain all the nutrition it can, and soup does just that. In addition, some of our elders do have a tooth problem: they just can't chew like they used to. So soup compensates for this. Or, if you have a pregnant cat who refuses milk, soup is the best method of getting milk to her. Use milk to make rich, creamy soups. This not only provides the vitamins and

*Soup should be warm, not hot.*

**If you have an old cat, soup is the perfect fireside feast.**

minerals which mother-to-be needs desperately, but it also provides the extra liquid she needs at this time.

Additional tips: you can make sure any vegetables are mashed enough by mashing them in your blender, if you have one. One way to make an excellent soup base for your cat is to use leftover steak or chicken bones. Cats love the base that comes from these delicacies.

All this information can help to make your pet a very chipper cat. If your cat looks as though he needs a little change in his life, get him all souped up with a little soup. He'll love it!

## VEGETABLE SOUP

*¼ pound hamburger*
*1 onion*
*1 carrot*
*1 can vegetable soup, drained*

Mash hamburger. Dice onion and carrot. Place meat, onion, and carrot in saucepan. Add vegetable soup. Cook until warm. Serve.

## BOUILLON THE BLUE HORIZON

*1 beef bouillon cube*
*1 cup water*
*2 tablespoons leftover meat*
*1 tablespoon leftover vegetables*

Dissolve bouillon in boiling water. Cut up meat. Mash vegetables and add to bouillon. Serve warm.

## EXTRA-ENERGY SOUP

*½ cup leftover meat*
*¼ can mushroom soup, undiluted*
*¼ cup milk*

Cut meat in small chunks. Warm with soup. Add milk just before serving. Place in bowl and serve.

## BACON SOUP

2 or 3 strips bacon
1 small jar strained baby food vegetables
¼ cup milk
2 tablespoons canned cat food

Cook bacon until crisp. Warm vegetables and milk. Place in bowl and mix with cat food. Top with crumbled bacon. Serve.

## LAMB SOUP

¼ pound lamb
1 small onion
Evaporated milk

Cut lamb into chunks. Dice onion. Combine in saucepan and simmer in some water (just enough to cover bottom of pan) about 10 minutes. Add some evaporated milk and serve.

## CHICKEN SOUP

¼ can cream of chicken soup, undiluted
1 small onion
½ green pepper
½ cup milk

Place chicken soup in saucepan. Dice onion and pepper. Add to chicken soup. Warm, adding milk to keep from burning. Serve in bowl.

## OLD-TIME PEA SOUP

1 small can split-pea soup, undiluted
Leftover meat (lamb, beef)
Catsup

Place pea soup in saucepan. Cut meat into chunks. Add to soup and warm. Add some catsup to color soup red and serve.

## CLAM CHOWDER FOR CATS

*1 onion*
*1 small can clam chowder, undiluted*
*Evaporated milk*
*Handful dry cat-food nuggets*

Slice onion. Place in saucepan with clam chowder. Add some evaporated milk. Warm. Mix with dry cat food. Serve.

## ONION SOUP SPECIAL

*1 cup water*
*1 package dry onion soup mix*
*¼ pound leftover meat (lamb, beef)*
*½ cup leftover spinach*

Boil water. Add soup mix and cook as directed on the package. Cut meat into chunks. Add to soup. Add spinach, mixing well. Serve.

## SHRIMPEE SOUP*

*1 onion*
*1 cup water*
*Leftover fresh shrimp*
*1 cup milk*
*Grated cheese*

Slice onion. Cook in water until soft. Shred shrimp. Add to onions. Add milk and warm. Top with cheese. Serve in bowl.

# 3

# Just for the Halibut!

*There's nothing like fresh fish.*

So your cat's been angling for some fish, eh? Let's face it—it's no great secret that fish is a feline favorite. A smart cat owner like you already knows this. So, just for the record, here are a few more words about fish for cats.

Of course there's nothing like fresh fish. Right off the boat. But sometimes "right off the boat" isn't fresh enough! I know a cat who went so far as to stow away on a deep-sea fishing jaunt with his master so he could be first in line for dinner!

Now no one is suggesting that every week you must go fishing to keep your pet playful, but if you are planning on a fresh-fish dinner for your family, you may want to save for your cat the bits and pieces of fish that accumulate as waste in the preparation of your own dinner. Or you may want to serve your cat any leftovers. So, at no extra cost, you can serve your cat such elegant treats as oysters, clams, crabmeat, lobster, or shrimp! And don't think this won't make for one happy cat. Why, after a fish dinner like this, he'll be the envy of any of those fancy uptown cats!

Say, what's all the picking and pawing? Is your cat dissatisfied? Well, if your cat is a finicky eater, the solution to the problem is quite simple. Cats love fish so much that if you mix some with other food he doesn't especially like, the bits of fish will lure him into eating it all. And by the way, fish shouldn't be served alone anyway. You see, it doesn't have the "filling power" that meat has. Your cat gets more miles to the gallon with meat than he does with

*Fish should not be served alone.*

fish. So let fish be the vehicle for feeding him other things that he may not like, but should have, for dinner.

O.K., just lie down on this couch and start talking. Ah-ha. So, that's it. Every time you make dinner for your cat he won't eat unless you give him fish? Very interesting. Well, listen: it doesn't take much knowledge of psychology to see that your cat knows a little about Freud. He knows that if he plays on your sympathy he can hold out for what *he* wants for dinner (fish, of course) rather than what you want to give him. Don't let him. If he starts to pull a few of his psychological tricks because he wants more fish, just give him small amounts of it, one out of every three meals, so that he'll be properly hungry for his meat meals.

And a word about canned fish for cats. Many of the commercial pet food companies make canned fish for cats. It's quite good. But, some authorities feel that if you use canned fish for cats in large quantities, your cat could develop urinary stones as he gets older, especially if he's an altered male, since canned fish for cats has a lot of calcium and ash in it. Cats need only a small amount of calcium and ash. Of course this varies from cat to cat. Ask your veterinarian for his opinion.

*Save some for the cat.*

Normally, there's nothing wrong with canned fish for cats if you don't give your pet too much of it. The pet food companies have teams of experts who supervise and regulate their recipes and the ingredients to government standards so that your cat is getting the same quality in each can. So there's no need for alarm. When it comes to canned fish for cats, suit yourself. Or ask your veterinarian. (Or ask your cat!)

Here are some helpful tips in preparing fish for your cat: all fish should be cooked before it is served. Some veterinarians feel that if you feed your cat raw fish in large amounts, it can lead to paralysis. Your own veterinarian can settle this controversy. (Of course you can feed your cat canned fish right from the can, since it has been cooked by the manufacturer.) Cod and flounder seem to be the most popular fish with cats. You can cook quite a large amount of fish at one time, break it into sections, then freeze it.

Then take small amounts from the freezer as needed. The top of a double boiler is suitable for thawing or warming it. Another trick is to let the fish thaw at room temperature, then, just before serving, pour boiling water over it.

You may want to cook fish by steaming it in a small amount of water, *au naturel*. Then shred it with your fingers before serving. This serves two purposes. It allows the fish to cool to the right temperature for eating (it should be warm, not hot), and it allows you to take the bones out. Yes, *remove the bones from all fish!* Remember: when it comes to fish for cats, *no bones allowed.*

Your cat may have a yen for fish pudding, which is both good and cheap. A quick method of preparing this delightful delicacy is by boiling a cod's head, removing it from the water and extracting the bones, then returning the head to the water, which has been thickened with bread or puppy biscuits.

The concentrated water (broth) that comes from cooking fish can be saved for your cat to drink. This way you can get your cat to drink fluids, if he's a teetotaler. Also, this broth can be used as a flavor tempter by pouring it over those foods he usually dislikes. Pretty sneaky, eh?

So next time you decide to give your cat a fish dinner, go to it!

*All fish should be cooked before serving it.*

*Remove the bones.*

Just open a can of fish for cats, or get out your bait and tackle the problem yourself. And if you do go fishing, your favorite pet won't mind one bit if you take him along, just for the halibut!

## FLOUNDER AROUND

*Fillets of flounder*
*Grated cheese*
*Margarine*
*Lemon juice*

Preheat broiler. Cover fillets with cheese and broil in margarine. Sprinkle few drops of lemon juice over fish and cheese. Broil about 4 minutes. Cut into small pieces. Allow to cool. Serve.

## FISH PUDDING*

*Leftover cooked fish*
*½ cup milk or water*
*½ cup bread crumbs or bread broken into pieces*

Shred fish. Warm in milk, adding bread until thick. Stir and cook about 2 minutes. Serve warm.

## SOUR CREAM FILLET

*¼ pound fish fillets (cod, flounder, haddock)*
*Margarine*
*Lemon*
*¼ cup sour cream*

Preheat broiler. Broil fish in margarine, sprinkling top with lemon. When done, mash with fork. Mix with sour cream in bowl and serve.

## FISH IN THE SEA

*¼ pound assorted fish (cod, flounder)*
*Leftover vegetables (stringbeans, spinach)*
*Margarine*
*¼ cup milk*

Mash fish and vegetables. Place in saucepan with a little margarine. Add milk. Heat, stirring frequently. Serve warm.

## TOAST OF THE TUNA

*1 slice toast*
*2 tablespoons leftover tuna salad*
*2 tablespoons cottage cheese*

Break up toast into small chunks. Mix with tuna salad and cottage cheese. Serve.

## SALAD A LA MER

*Leftover assorted fish (tuna, salmon, sardines)*
*2 tablespoons cottage cheese*
*1 hard-cooked egg*
*Grated cheese*

Mash fish. Mix with cottage cheese and sliced egg. Sprinkle grated cheese on top. Serve.

## SARDINE SANDWICH

*Leftover sardines with oil*
*2 strips bacon*

Mash sardines in oil. Cook bacon. Surround sardines with bacon.
Serve.

## CRABMEAT SPECIAL

*Surplus crabmeat or lobster bits*
*1 teaspoon catsup*
*1 hard-cooked egg*

Mash crabmeat. Mix with catsup. Slice egg and mix with fish. Serve.

## CREAMED SHRIMP STEW*

*Surplus shrimp*
*½ cup milk*
*1 slice margarine*
*Handful dry cat food*

Shred shrimp. Place shrimp and milk in saucepan or double boiler.
Add margarine. Heat, stirring constantly. Add handful of dry cat
food. Serve.

## CANTON TUNA

*2 tablespoons tuna for cats*
*2 teaspoons Chinese vegetables*
*Margarine*

Mix and mash tuna and vegetables. Melt some margarine and pour
over mixture. Serve.

# 4

# Rough Rough (for Smooth Cats)!

*There comes a time when just about everything is unbearable.*

There comes a time in every cat's life when just about everything is unbearable. He feels grumpy. Grouchy. Listless. Nothing seems to pull him out of his lethargy. Even catnip doesn't count!

One reason for this listlessness, fellow cat lovers, could be constipation. (Naturally, there could be many other reasons, much more serious, and you'd be wise to have your cat see his vet.) Obviously, if friend feline is feeling filled up these days, and can't do anything about it, *you* must help.

One of the best ways to aid in keeping your cat's insides clean, is to make sure he gets some starchy vegetables, or roughage, in his dinner. He needs roughage. It makes him smooth. Some of the vegetables recommended by veterinarians are: cabbage, raw carrots (diced and mashed), peas, parsnips, corn (either creamed or corn-on-the-cob), and string beans. In addition to its value as a proper laxative, roughage adds variety to his meals. And cats need variety. Now there's nothing wrong, actually, with feeding your cat the same food every day, providing you feed him a balanced diet, but he does need the addition of roughage for variety. Variety in his diet, and in his individual meals, insures that his appetite will not be dulled. Don't set the same old plate of the same old food before him too often, or you'll find that you have one glum cat on your hands!

This doesn't mean that you should place a heaping bowlful of spinach in front of your pet cat, but the method of including starchy vegetables recommended by most authorities is to mix them right in with his other food.

And mix them well! There are two reasons for this: cats, somewhat like their canine counterparts, don't chew very well. You see, a human's back teeth (molars) are not as pointed as a cat's. We use our molars to grind and mash food, preparing it for the action of the digestive juices in our stomachs. But our feline friends just rip and tear at their food, with a minimum of chewing, and they swallow food in whole chunks rather than masticating it. A cat's digestive juices are very strong, and they can easily disintegrate the hardiest of food. If a cat swallows a bone, it will be soft in about an hour, because of his strong digestive juices. But the one difference between the cat and us humans is that, even though his digestive juices are quite strong, there's not enough *ptyalin* in his juices to act effec-

*You may have to resort to camouflage and trickery.*

tively on starch. Ptyalin is an enzyme found in human saliva. It helps us digest starch. Cats have very little ptyalin. So you must thoroughly cook or mash starchy vegetables before you mix them with his meal.

Secondly, you may have to resort to camouflage and trickery to get your feline to feast off a meal festooned with starchy vegetables. Let's face it. Even though spinach may be good for us, there are some of us who don't like it. The same is true with cats. There are some vegetables your cat may hate, even though they're good for him. So mix the starchy roughage in with his meal, and do it cleverly. Another aspect of camouflaging vegetables in with his meal is that as a cat becomes more domesticated, he is not able to provide for himself as well as he could when he was wild. Animal instinct in respect to feeding is usually pretty good, except when that animal is domesticated. When a cat is wild, he eats mice and other living things, skin, tail, ears, and all, which provide the roughage he needs to keep him smooth and lubricated internally. But with highly domestic cats, *you* must provide roughage for him. In addition, as a cat becomes domesticated, he loses his taste for natural roughage and you must sometimes force him into including some in his dinner. So mash and mix. *And* hide it! Simple?

*There are some of us who just don't like spinach.*

*Mew Mew Gai Pan*

You see, basically the cat is omnivorous rather than carnivorous or herbivorous. He needs a balance of both meat and vegetables. When he catches a mouse, and eats it, in a sense he's eating vegetables. Roughage. How? Because the mouse is herbivorous, and along with the meaty flesh of the mouse, your cat gets the benefit of the vitamins and minerals derived from the vegetables in the stomach and intestine of the rodent.

By cooking starches completely for your cat, you promote the process known as cracking open or breaking down the starch granules. What happens is that the granules swell, due to moisture in the raw material. When you cook them, they burst, which makes them easier for your cat to digest.

Even if you include raw, leafy vegetables in your feline's food, make sure to shred and mix them well.

Here are a few things to remember when you prepare starchy vegetables for your cat: spinach, Brussels sprouts, onions, white potatoes, broccoli tips, asparagus tips, beets, cabbage, and string beans are all loved by cats. You may want to substitute rice for a vegetable. Make sure, though, that it is thoroughly cooked. Or you can add, as a substitute, the juice of a few carrots or tomatoes. Also in the starch category are macaroni and noodles, which cats love. Remember that usually the prescribed ratio between meat and vegetables is three to one. If your cat's dinner totals four ounces, there should be three ounces of meat and one ounce of vegetables, mixed in (roughly 1 teaspoonful). Here's a tip on how to camouflage a much-needed, but often-disliked, food in your cat's dinner. When preparing to give your cat cabbage, mash it and mix it with a very moist meal (almost soupy) so that your cat won't be able to pick out the bits and pieces he likes and leave the cabbage behind.

So if you're heading for the kitchen to prepare dinner for your cat, don't forget roughage. It will help him be a regular fellow. The point is, my pets, if you want your cat to be an old smoothie, feed him starchy vegetables. He needs them!

## CARROT CARESS

*1 carrot, cooked*
*1 teaspoon beef*
*Milk*

Mash carrot. Sauté beef for about 2 minutes. Mix carrots and meat, topping with some milk which is at room temperature. Serve in bowl.

## BELLE LE CAT

*3 teaspoons dry breakfast cereal, unsugared*
*Milk*
*1 egg*

Put rice or wheat cereal in bowl. Add some warm milk to raw egg and beat well. Add milk and egg mixture to cereal so that cereal just becomes moist. Mix and mash well. Serve in bowl.

## CAT SPAW

*Leftover chicken, boned*
*Milk*
*Small amount leftover cabbage*

Mash chicken well. Add just enough warm milk to moisten chicken. Add small amount of warm leftover cabbage. Mix well. Serve in bowl.

## LOUIS CAT ORZE

*Small amount leftover spinach*
*1 teaspoon leftover beef, chicken, or lamb*
*Dry cat food.*

Warm spinach and mash. Combine spinach with meat. Add handful of dry cat food. Serve in bowl.

## THE CAT'S PAJAMAS (LATE NIGHT SNACK)

*1 raw egg*
*Small amount of milk*
*2 teaspoons wheat germ*

Mix raw egg with milk. Warm. Add wheat germ. Serve in bowl.

## PUSSY CAFE

*Beef kidney*
*2 teaspoons canned cat food*
*2 teaspoons leftover spinach*
*Milk*

Cut up raw beef kidney into small pieces. Mix with canned cat food. Add warm spinach and mix well. Pour warm milk over ingredients. Serve in bowl.

## QUICK LUNCH

*3 ounces chopped meat*
*1 teaspoon leftover string beans*
*Garlic powder*

Mash meat with fork. Warm string beans, dice and combine with meat, mixing well. Sprinkle with garlic powder. Serve in bowl.

## HENRI CAT

 *1 raw carrot, diced*
 *2 or 3 teaspoons canned cat food*
 *¼ cup chicken, bacon, or beef gravy*

Mix carrot with cat food. Warm gravy. Pour over rest of ingredients. Serve in bowl.

## NOODLE DROODLE

 *2 ounces macaroni or noodles*
 *Chopped meat*
 *Beef gravy*

Cook noodles as directed on package. Make sure they're soft. Mash well. Combine with raw chopped meat. Place in bowl. Pour warm gravy over meal. Serve.

## MEW MEW GAI PAN

 *Small amount leftover fish, boned*
 *2 ounces instant rice, cooked*
 *Small amount tomato juice*
 *Garlic powder*

Place fish in bowl. Add warm instant rice. Mix well. Top with juice and garlic powder. Serve.

# 5

# Two Fingers' Worth—and No Ice, Please

*His drinking should be done in moderation.*

No one wants to dampen your cat's fun, but let's face it, his drinking should be done in moderation. Drinking of milk, that is. Nothing can spoil your cat's future—or his stomach—faster than too many bouts with the milk bottle. Of course there is a great difference between "a couple of belts with the boys" and a delirious binge in the back room. Unless you're absolutely sure how much milk your cat can drink without exceeding his limit, then be careful how much you put in his saucer. Just about two fingers' worth (and without ice, please) will do it!

A drink of milk can hit your cat all of a sudden, and since it takes a while for the milk to get into and through his system, he may not feel the punch until a while after he's had quite a few laps. And then —*pow!* He's headed for the potty. You see, many cats have trouble digesting milk. It acts as a powerful laxative for a great number of them, so if they drink too much, they get awfully loose!

Another thing that can sober you up fast is the danger of calcium in milk. Milk has a high calcium content. Now that's just fine for kittens. They need calcium to promote bone formation and growth, but altered adults and old cats can react differently. They've stopped growing. Some veterinarians feel that if they drink too much milk, the calcium can form deposits in their systems and lead to many a disease of old age. Not to mention difficulty in walking a straight line!

For many cat owners it's hard to believe that milk is not *the* complete food for cats. A large number of novice cat owners will substitute milk for water as the liquid part of the cat's diet. This doesn't make sense. If a cat drinks a lot of milk every day, he'll need very little other food. Cats live on about 300–400 calories a day. And this

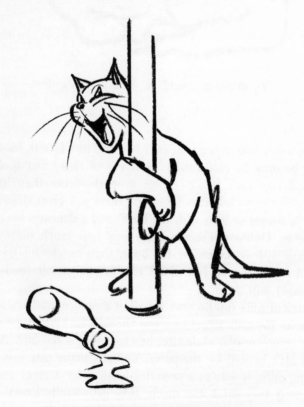

*Don't let him become a problem drinker.*

*If your cat is very constipated, give him all the milk he can drink.*

is the amount in a pint of milk. Some cats would chug-a-lug a pint of milk a day, given the opportunity. (Of course this is not usually the case!) And if he eats other food, he's going to be an awfully fat cat!

Another problem is that if your cat goes on a milk binge, you may have trouble getting him to eat solid food. Even a strait jacket won't help! So try not to let your cat get so hooked on milk that he becomes a problem drinker.

No matter how much or how little milk you give your cat, he must have fresh water at paw at all times. It's an excellent chaser! It helps carry away many of the body's waste materials. The important thing to remember about water is that it must be fresh, clean, and convenient!

Of course there's nothing wrong with milk for your cat if it's served in moderation. After all, milk helps to balance your cat's diet and keep him regular without the use of laxatives. Naturally if your cat is very constipated and has been straining (to get at the milk bowl), don't hold him back. Give him all the milk he can drink.

Obviously milk has a lot of protein in it, but if you want to add protein to your cat's diet without falling prey to the laxative qual-

*Milk should be a little warm before serving.*

ities of milk, here's a simple tip. Put your kitten on the cheese! That's right, my pets, cheese is a terrific substitute for milk. No one advocates that your cat should be served a little triangle of Gruyère and crackers with his coffee, but if your pet gets any of the soft, bland cheeses he'll be perfectly satisfied. Cream cheese, cottage cheese, and farmer's cheese are particular favorites.

A few parting thoughts about milk for your cat: milk should always be a little warm before serving. Warm it up for just a few seconds in a saucepan. Or let it come to room temperature. *Never serve your cat milk right from the refrigerator!* Fresh milk is less laxative than evaporated milk, although many cats prefer the canned stuff. In the summer you may want to give your cat powdered milk or skim milk, since cats require less fat then.

Milk is generally good for your cat and an important part of his diet. But before you and your pet sit down and have one for the road, remember: have only one! He's got a limit!

# 6

# Breed Between the Lines!

*If he's too fat, the girls won't give him a second look.*

If you're the lucky cat owner who has a purebred pet, you're quite aware that you must stick to the bloodlines in order to produce kittens that carry on the breed. Selective breeding has produced fine specimens of cats that are the fun and joy of any owner. But if you own a cat who comes from a very "ordinary" background you don't have to be as selective in breeding your pet—you can breed between the lines! And still you can have a pet who brings joy to your household. So, if you have an ordinary male cat and you can't stop him from living the life of a Park Avenue playboy, just prepare yourself to give your roving Romeo all the nourishment he can get. He needs it!

The most important element in the amorous male's diet is meat. And the good stuff, too. This is one of the few times in his life when you should give him a little raw beef. Beef will make him strong. And, if we believe popular superstition, it will make him anxious! So if you don't want him to be ashamed of his performance, give him raw beef. And not too fat, either! The trimmer the meat, the trimmer the cat! After all, if he's too fat, the girls won't give him a second look as he runs along the fence!

Let's face it, some female cats are particular "types." First of all,

*Some female cats are particular "types."*

there's the possessive type. She spends one evening with your male cat, then starts spreading the rumor around the alley that she is your cat's big heart throb of the year. Then there's the catty type. Her sharp-tongued sarcasm leaves no room for a pleasant word about anyone. Of course every cat has run into the extra-popular girl cat who's booked solid several weeks in advance. And then there's always the shy type or the good-sport type, both of whom won't let him get to first base!

With all of these frustrating types of femininity plus the exhaus-

*Then there's always the shy type . . .*

*Fun-loving normal cats*

tion which comes from his relations with fun-loving normal cats, your male charmer can become quite tired! He's going through an awful lot just to satisfy his desires. So make sure he eats regularly as well as properly. You may want to put him back onto a three-meal-a-day plan of smaller, but effective, meals. Concentrate on meat, eggs, cottage cheese, fish, and liver. These are all protein foods, which will help him get through the night without being too tuckered out.

If you have an ordinary female cat who's ripe for a little fancy paw holding, you must also be careful of her diet. She'll need an abundance of nourishing food especially to build her up to handle the strain she must go through in bearing kittens. Again, beef and the protein foods are especially helpful.

If you have an altered adult male or a spayed female, whose sex drive has been sublimated, you may find that the sublimation takes form in the drive for food. Many "fixed" cats will drown their desires in an orgy of bowl licking! This means that you should be careful that your de-sexed cat doesn't get too fat. The object is to feed him the quantity of food that will keep him in proper health without adding weight.

Now that your pet has become the most popular cat in the neighborhood, the most important thing is his stamina, and feeding him properly helps him maintain stamina. Remember this, and there's no doubt that your cat will be popular for a long time to come!

*He's going through an awful lot just to satisfy his desires.*

## ON-THE-FENCE FRICASSEE

> *2 ounces liver (beef, chicken)*
> *Margarine*
> *1 hard-cooked egg*
> *2 teaspoons cottage cheese*

Cut liver into small pieces. Sauté in margarine. Cut egg into small pieces. Mix liver and egg with cottage cheese. Serve.

## SALMON SURPRISE

> *2 tablespoons leftover salmon*
> *¼ cup milk*
> *2 tablespoons cottage cheese*
> *Handful dry cat food*

Mash salmon. Mix with milk. Add cottage cheese and mix well. Sprinkle with dry cat food. Serve.

## ALL BEEFED UP!*

*1 tablespoon flour*
*1 tablespoon margarine*
*½ cup milk*
*3 ounces beef*
*1 teaspoon leftover vegetables (carrots, string beans, spinach)*

Stir flour into melted margarine until thick paste is formed. Add milk. Cook until smooth, about 1 minute, stirring constantly. Cut up and mash beef. Add to flour and milk mixture. Mash vegetables and mix in. Serve warm.

## CHICKEN MADRID

*2 ounces chicken liver*
*½ small onion*
*1 teaspoon leftover carrots*
*1 teaspoon leftover string beans*

Cut liver into small pieces. Cut onion, carrots, and warm with string beans. Mix liver with vegetables and serve.

## LIVER MAGNIFICENT

*2 ounces chicken liver*
*2 eggs*
*1 teaspoon wheat germ*

Cut up raw chicken liver. Boil eggs 4 minutes. Mix with liver. Sprinkle on wheat germ. Serve.

## SARDINE SUPREME

*Leftover sardines in oil*
*Dry cat food*
*¼ small onion*

Chop sardines into small pieces and place in bowl with oil. Add handful dry cat food. Dice onion and mix well. Serve.

## LOVER'S QUICK LUNCH*

> ½ cup leftover meat
> 2 tablespoons leftover vegetables
> ½ slice toast
> ¼ onion
> Milk

Cut meat, vegetables, toast, and onion into bite-sized chunks. Place in bowl. Top with just enough milk to make mixture moist. Serve.

## VEAL ROBERTO*

> Leftover veal scaloppine
> Margarine
> 1 tablespoon red wine
> Grated Italian cheese

Cut veal into pieces. Sauté in margarine 30 seconds. Place in bowl. Add wine. Top with few sprinkles of cheese. Serve.

## LAMB DE LUXE

> 3 tablespoons leftover lamb
> 1 teaspoon cooking oil
> Salt
> 1 tablespoon sour cream

Cut lamb into pieces. Rub with oil. Add a little salt. Mix with sour cream. Serve.

## JUICY BURGER

> 1 ounce evaporated milk
> 2 ounces ground raw beef
> Grated cheese

Mix milk with beef. Top with grated cheese. Serve.

# 7

# Full Womb and Empty Arms

*So your cat is going to have kittens!*

So your cat is going to have kittens! Congratulations. Well, when the expectant mother is standing there with a full womb and empty arms, you'll want to plan her meals with a little tender, loving care. So lend an ear.

Obviously, the main thing to remember is that Mother needs wholesome, but not fattening, food. After all, with the load that's on her mind, there's no need adding the extra burden of calorie counting.

But she does need *more* food now that she has more than herself to feed, so you may want to feed her three small meals a day rather than her usual two. Of course there's no need to rush into the kitchen as soon as she tells you that she's going to be a mother, but now is the time when you must consider her nourishment of prime importance.

One of the interesting sidelights about a cat's food intake during pregnancy is that she, like human mothers-to-be, develops strange cravings. You may even find her wanting to munch on an appetizer of soap! So if she starts raving for her cravings, you'll know exactly what to expect out of her one of these fine days!

Her regular meals should be carefully selected to provide maximum nourishment. Plenty of meat, eggs, fish (a little more than usual), and milk should be the basic ingredients of meal planning for the expectant mother. And, by the way, when you do give your bulging

*Like human mothers-to-be, she develops strange cravings!*

female cat milk, probably the best kind is sweetened condensed milk. Why? Because sweetened condensed milk contains more amounts of vitamins A and D than does fresh cow's milk. And, let's face it, she needs vitamins.

It stands to reason that she needs a little more liquid in her diet than she usually gets. After all, she must make all the milk for the new family, and she needs plenty of liquid in her to do it. There's no need to worry about forcing her to drink, though. You see, Mother Nature has already taken care of that. Your pregnant cat will more than likely be thirstier than usual, and she'll gladly accept any liquid you pour her way.

Of course, if she's the exception to the rule, one way to insure that she gets enough liquids in her diet is to give her more "sloppy" foods, like soup. Another way is to include carrot juice (a particular favorite among cats) and green vegetables in her meat meals.

If you want your cat to be especially prolific, it is generally assumed that you should feed her raw food rather than cooked. Laboratory tests have shown that if a female gets raw food she'll produce large squadrons of kittens. Conversely, it has also been substantiated in the labs that females who eat only cooked food often die while giving birth. Of course, this doesn't apply to all females, and probably not to your lovely feline!

During the last week before the expected birth, make sure Mother's

*She may want to play Greta Garbo, demanding to be left alone.*

natural functions remain natural. This is important. Give her foods that tend to be laxative. You see, if she's constipated she may have trouble giving birth, not to mention having trouble passing her after-birth. If she does get constipated around this time, or has a loss of appetite, it's worth a call to your friendly veterinarian for remedial instructions or advice.

When the time comes for her to start the assembly lines rolling, you may want to remember these few hints. The day before the birth, the mother may want to play Greta Garbo, demanding to be left alone. This is quite normal and should not cause you to worry. Also, she may refuse dinner immediately before birth. There's no cause for concern here, either. Let's face it—she's about to go on stage for a command performance, so let her have her own way!

If, after the arrivals have appeared, the mother is worn out, let her step back and admire her work for a little while. With the pro-duction she's been through, she has a right to be proud! So let her rest for an hour or so, then give her a good meal. One excellent suggestion for a nourishing meal is a couple of eggs beaten up in a little warm milk. Or, you may want to reward her for her efforts by putting a little sugar in the milk. The sugar will help to give her the energy she needs at this delicate moment.

If she fails to lick her babies after their arrival, or she seems to

*Give her five to ten drops of brandy or gin in a little milk. This ought to bring her around to her old self again!*

be in pain, give her five to ten drops of brandy or gin in a little milk. This ought to bring her around to her old self again!

Well, now that the new mama has safely emptied her womb of its passengers, you can fill up your arms with the new cuddly, furry kittens. They're going to be fun to have around!

## EGG AND SPINACH CASCADE

> *2 teaspoons leftover spinach*
> *2 hard-cooked eggs*
> *1 teaspoon margarine*
> *½ cup milk*
> *Grated cheese*

Warm spinach topped with margarine. Slice eggs. Mix eggs with spinach in cat bowl. Add milk and top with a few sprinkles of grated cheese. Serve.

## AFTER-DELIVERY APERITIF

> *½ cup condensed milk*
> *½ teaspoon sugar*
> *Few drops brandy or gin*

Warm milk. Stir in sugar. Add brandy or gin and stir. Serve in bowl.

## CHEESE, PLEASE!

*½ cup creamed cottage cheese*
*¼ small can chicken parts for cats*
*3 or 4 soda crackers*

Mix cottage cheese with canned cat food. Top with crumbled soda crackers. Serve in bowl.

## MEAT DE LUXE

*4 ounces leftover meat*
*2 eggs*
*1 slice toast*

Cut up meat into bite-sized chunks. Place in bowl. Boil eggs 4 minutes. Add eggs to meat. Crumble toast and add. Serve.

## SALAD JAXIN

*Leftover meat*
*½ small onion*
*⅛ cup leftover string beans*
*¼ small green pepper*
*Margarine*

Cut meat into small chunks. Mince onion, string beans, pepper. Warm vegetables in margarine. Mix vegetables with meat in cat bowl and serve.

## FISH NEAPOLITAN

*1 leftover fish fillet (flounder, cod, sole)*
*½ small onion*
*½ cup tomato sauce*
*Garlic salt*

Cut up fillet into chunks. Mince onion. Warm fish and onion in tomato sauce. Add some garlic salt. Serve in bowl.

## TOMATO TREAT FOR CATS

*½ cup creamed cottage cheese*
*1 hard-cooked egg*
*1 small tomato*
*¼ cup milk*

Place cottage cheese in cat bowl. Cut up egg and tomato into small bits. Mix in with cottage cheese. Add milk and serve.

## CHICKEN LICKIN'

*3 ounces cut-up leftover chicken*
*½ small onion*
*½ carrot*
*1 teaspoon mayonnaise or salad dressing*

Place chicken in bowl. Mince onion and carrot, and add to chicken. Add mayonnaise or salad dressing and mix well. Serve.

## SHRIMP SCRAMBLE

*2 eggs*
*Leftover shrimp*
*Handful cat nuggets*

Boil eggs 4 minutes. Place in bowl. Cut shrimp into small pieces. Add to eggs. Top with cat nuggets. Serve.

## SUMMER CHEESE

*Chunks of your cat's favorite fresh fruit*
*¼ cup creamed cottage cheese*

Cut fruit into small pieces. Mix with cheese. Serve in bowl.

# 8

# Udder Delight!

*Mama is now the main source of food for her always-hungry brood.*

Want to make sure that the new kittens will get all the milk they need? Here are a few things to know when cooking for the lactating cat.

The most important thing to remember is that Mama is now the main souce of food for her always-hungry brood. So she must be well fed in order to feed her kittens well!

Obviously the new mother must also remain strong. Therefore, any food that keeps her strong enough to pacify her audience of wide-open mouths is to her benefit. The most advantageous foods for the lactating cat seem to be raw minced beef, eggs, fish, and, of course, milk.

Although Mom will probably be ravenous after her ordeal of producing the new kittens, many authorities contend that, after her initial hunger is satisfied, she should be fed in moderation. Then, gradually, her meals should increase in quantity so that she can be a good provider for her litter. The reason for this is that although the kittens will be living primarily on milk, and *her* milk to be exact, they won't demand that much from her for the first few days. Then they'll start getting so hungry that she had better be ready for them when they start screeching to an anxious halt at the filling station!

Generally speaking, while nursing her babies the lactating mother should eat four or five meals per day. After all, the more kittens

*A healthy cat will have four or five kittens.*

she has, the more food she requires. And make each meal small but effective. Milk, milk by-products, and beef should be the mainstays.

A healthy cat will have four or five kittens in one litter. If you shy off at having that many kittens around the house, you may want to farm them out to suitable foster homes. It's best to wait until the kittens are weaned before you separate them from Mom. Of course, you can give them away almost immediately, but, if you do, make sure that there's at least one kitten left in the litter for Mom to nurse. Or else she may not be able to eliminate the large milk supply she's accumulated.

There are times when you are faced with the possibility of arranging for a foster mother for the new brood. If the mother dies, or she's not well enough to feed her babies, or she doesn't have enough milk herself, you may be forced to start searching for a substitute. When you do find one, you must include your kittens in with hers. The foster mother must be bluffed into thinking that all the kittens in her care are her own products. So you may want to try a few commando tactics. Mix the kittens in with hers in the

*The foster mother must be bluffed into thinking the kittens are her own.*

dark, or when she's away. You may be able to add only one or two kittens so that she doesn't end up with too many mouths draining her supply. You may try to withdraw one of her own kittens as you add one of yours. This way she'll be bluffed into thinking they're her own. In order to get the foster mother to accept her new responsibilities, you must get her to lick the new kittens. How? Smear the kittens with butter and the mother will gladly lick them. The reason for getting her to lick them is to start an emotional tie between Mother and baby, and she must be bluffed into lowering her resistance to any obvious strangers. Once she licks them, she's licked!

A parting thought: make sure you take especially good care of Mama during these few weeks. Patience, common sense, and kind-

*Smear the kittens with butter . . .*

*Once she licks them, she's licked!*

*Make sure you take good care of Mama.*

ness are necessary attitudes in cooking and caring for her. Utilizing these basic ideas, you should find that your lactating cat has no trouble being an udder delight to her kittens.

## MR. MILKTOAST

*¼ cup milk*
*1 egg*
*1 slice toast*

Warm milk. Beat raw egg in milk. Break up toast into small pieces. Place in bottom of cat bowl and pour milk mixture over it. Serve.

## MEAT 'N' MUSHROOM CLASH

*¼ can cream of mushroom soup, undiluted*
*Leftover meat*

Warm mushroom soup. Cut meat into small pieces. Add to soup and serve in bowl.

## GENERAL CUSTARD

*¼ cup milk*
*1 teaspoon vanilla custard powder*
*Canned cat food*

Warm milk. Add custard powder and stir for 1 minute, making sure it's dissolved. Add to cat food and serve.

## TRACK-MEAT TEMPTER

*½ small can condensed milk*
*½ hard-cooked egg*
*2 teaspoons raw beef*

Place condensed milk in bowl. Cut up egg and meat into small pieces and mix well. Add to milk. Serve.

## EGG 'N' FLOW BRUNCH

*1 graham cracker*
*¼ cup milk*
*1 egg*
*Grated cheese*

Crumble graham cracker into milk so that mixture becomes mushy. Mix in raw egg. Top with grated cheese. Serve.

## HI-FI TUNA

¼ *cup creamed cottage cheese*
¼ *cup tuna for cats*
1 *hard-cooked egg*

Mix cheese with tuna. Cut egg into small pieces. Mix in with fish mixture and serve in bowl.

## SUMMER SCRAMBLE

3 *teaspoons beef kidney*
¼ *cup sour cream*
*Grated cheese*

Cut fresh kidney into bite-sized pieces. Place in bowl. Add sour cream. Top with grated cheese. Serve.

## NORWEGIAN INTERLUDE

¼ *cup creamed cottage cheese*
2 *soda crackers*
*Oil from can of sardines*

Place cheese in bowl. Break soda crackers into bite-sized pieces. Mix with cottage cheese. Pour in sardine oil (just enough to moisten) and serve.

## FANCY LIVER

*Small amount chicken or calf's liver*
*Margarine*
*Sour cream*

Cut up liver in small pieces. Sauté in margarine. Add to sour cream and mix well. Serve.

## RAINBOW FISH

*Leftover bits and pieces of crabmeat, lobster, or shrimp from
    your own dinner*
*Catsup*
*Lemon juice*
*Soda crackers*

Mix fish with some catsup, add some lemon juice. Break soda
crackers into small pieces and add to mixture. Serve in bowl.

# 9

# Feed the Kitty

*Five feedings a day isn't as much as it seems.*

None of you back-room poker players needs to worry when it comes time to ante up and feed the kitty! Feeding your kitten is a lot easier than you think.

Generally speaking, the best food your kitten can have is the milk his mother gives him. That's because the fat content of the normal dam's milk is just right. During the first three weeks of the new kitten's life, he'll live exclusively off the fat of the dam! By the end of the third week any food you can persuade him to eat will help mother regain her strength and stamina for the job of her baby's post-natal education. At this time, naturally, a substitute mother must take over the job of feeding. Who? Why, you, of course!

There are other complications, though. You may be faced with the problem of feeding a whole brood of orphan kittens right from their birth. You see, the milk of some mothers is not satisfying enough, and the kittens must have some outside help. Or the mother may die in childbirth, leaving a whole basketful of screaming orphans for you to nurse. In any event, you must take over the complete job.

The most difficult thing to determine is the amount of food to give the new kittens. The wisest thing to do, if you're a novice, is to consult your veterinarian. He can give you the sound advice and the firm reassurance you need at this time.

Usually a kitten that is a few days old will gladly settle for five to ten c.c.s of milk five times a day. A c.c. is usually about the quantity you'd find in a medicine dropper. Five c.c.s are the equivalent of about one teaspoon of milk. The milk should be warm, not hot. Never feed your kitten, or full-grown cat, for that matter, milk right out of the refrigerator.

Five feedings a day isn't as much as it seems. You can feed your starving kitty in the morning right before your own breakfast, for his first meal, then again at midmorning for a second meal. Shortly after your own lunch, by early afternoon, he's ready for another swig of milk for his third meal. Around teatime, during the late afternoon, fill him up again. Finally, just after your own dinner, give him his fifth meal. Chances are, your kitty will not bother you during the night for another meal, if you can manage to get in all these feedings during the day. See? Simple, isn't it? Of course you may have an extremely ravenous kitten who may demand a non-alcoholic nightcap, but don't fret if he does. After all, he's growing up and he needs filling up!

After the first few days you can probably adjust his meals to the

*Now is the time to start adding supplement to your kitten's meals.*

more normal four-a-day plan. By the fourth week, your kitten should be getting foods more substantial than just milk. If he has been fed by Mama up to this point, you may want to start him off on his new diet by shredding some finely ground meat, especially beef (see "Meat Me for Dinner, Baby"), and giving it to him for a special meal. Your kitten should like it, and his mother will really like you. If your little kitty is normal, he will want more and more meat day by day. The increase in quantity is noticeable by the end of the fourth week.

Now is the time when you should start adding supplement to your kitten's meals. Start him with a little strained baby food mixed with meat. As he gets older you may want to add wheat germ or shredded wheat finely chopped. By the sixth week, which is usually weaning time, your kitten will be used to eating solid food in addition to milk. The kittens are ready to eat a number of foods that will add variety and nourishment to their growing bodies. Eggs, cottage cheese, steamed fish, spinach, and soups are all foods that famished felines favor.

Does your kitty look as though he's about to drill for oil? Well, he doesn't have to act like John Paul Getty for you to know that oil is essential for his well-being. Cod-liver oil, that is. Or, halibut oil.

*Oil is essential to their well-being.*

Why oil? Cod-liver oil is an essential source of vitamin D—the "sunshine" vitamin. A drop of oil every day, especially for a city kitty who must live in an apartment and cannot get the benefit of a good romp outside, is essential in preventing rickets. Also, oil allows bone formation and general growth of the skeleton to progress normally.

How much do you feed your kitten? The rule of thumb is that not only must the kitten's appetite be satisfied, but he must have enough to make sure his body is growing as it should—rapidly. After weaning, kittens are still to eat five meals per day, *not* counting milk. One or two of these meals should be meat or meat and a supplement. The meat should be raw or cooked beef. No one meal should be too large. First of all, you'll give your cat indigestion before his time. And, if any one meal is too large, he'll stuff himself and won't show any interest in the next meal. So keep them suitable, simple, and sufficient. At three months, kittens should have four

*Put some butter or margarine in the bottom of the bowl.*

meals per day, of about two or three ounces per meal. Over four months, you can feed him as much food as you'd give your altered adult cat. Of course, this means that he gets as much food *per day* as the adult, not per meal. Remember: you're feeding your kitty more often, since each individual meal is smaller than the adult cat would get. This point to remember is that *each meal is to be digested before the next begins!* By the time your kitty is five or six months old, he will start eating more at each meal, which means that it will take longer to digest dinner; thus cut down on the number of meals to three. When he reaches nine months, or adulthood, he's ready to live on two good meals a day, plus a possible saucer of milk at breakfast.

Here are some tips on feeding your kitten. Beat an egg in some body-temperature milk for a late-night snack for your kitten. Egg yolk is a good source of vitamin A. If your kitten is an orphan and refuses to drink milk from a saucer when you first get him, he probably is frightened of his new home. Don't force him to eat. When he gets hungry he'll be glad to make a dive for the food bowl. If you must feed him yourself, try a baby bottle or a medicine dropper to get the milk into his mouth. He'll probably resist you a little at first, but when the warm milk he inherently craves starts cascading down his throat, he'll forget where he is, what you're doing to him, and why he's angry. All attention will be focused on filling his tummy.

One way to start your kitten eating from a bowl (usually they have no trouble) is by putting some butter or margarine in the bottom of the bowl. As he begins to lick the bottom, start pouring milk right into the bowl. He'll get the idea!

You see, feeding your kitten isn't all that difficult. Just a little common sense and patience go a long way. So put down those poker chips, Mom, it's time to feed the kitty!

These recipes are for the weaned kitten. They are arranged so that the first few are for the kitten that has only recently been weaned, while the remainder are for older kittens.

## CRACKER, JACK!

*1 egg*
*Milk*
*3 soda crackers*

Beat egg and milk together. Warm just to take off chill. Pour in bowl. Crumble soda crackers in milk and egg mixture. Serve.

## FORMULA NO. 2

*½ cup milk*
*1 egg*
*½ teaspoon corn syrup*

Warm milk and egg to body temperature (test with elbow). Add corn syrup. Mix well. Serve in bowl.

## YOU WOULDN'T KIDNEY, WOULD YOU?*

*2 teaspoons beef kidney*
*1 teaspoon leftover vegetables*
*1 teaspoon canned cat food*

Cut raw kidney into small chunks. Warm vegetables in saucepan. Combine with prepared cat food in cat bowl. Mix well. Serve.

## FORT KNOX SURPRISE

*1 bouillon cube*
*½ cup warm water*
*1 hard-boiled egg*
*1 teaspoon chopped beef*

Melt bouillon in water. Cut up egg into small pieces. Separate meat into small chunks. Mix egg with meat in cat bowl. Pour bouillon over mixture. Serve warm.

## BEEF SEGUE

2 teaspoons chopped beef
½ teaspoon wheat germ
Milk

Separate chopped beef into small chunks. Place in bowl. Add wheat germ and then milk. Serve.

## KITTEN ON THE CHEESE

1 teaspoon spinach
1 teaspoon fish
1 teaspoon cottage cheese

Warm spinach. Shred fish into small pieces and add cottage cheese. Add spinach. Blend together. Serve in bowl.

## KITTEN CRUNCH

2 teaspoons leftover fish
2 ounces milk
Handful of cornflakes

Mince fish. Warm with milk in saucepan. Place cornflakes in bowl and add fish and milk mixture. Serve.

## RED TOP RAMBLE

2 teaspoons leftover carrots
1 teaspoon cornflakes
Milk

Mash carrots. Add cornflakes and mix well. Place in bowl. Warm milk in saucepan. Mix in with carrots and cornflakes. Serve warm.

## LEAN BABY BRUNCH

> 2 teaspoons raw or cooked beef
> ½ teaspoon wheat germ
> 1 egg
> 1 teaspoon strained baby vegetables

Shred meat. Mix with egg. Blend in wheat germ and strained vegetables. Serve in bowl.

## MORNING DELIGHT

> 1 teaspoon strained baby vegetables
> 2 teaspoons chopped beef
> Milk

Warm vegetables. Separate meat into small chunks. Mix vegetables with meat in bowl and top with milk. Serve.

# 10
## Senior Citizens

*Perhaps the kindest thing you can do for your cat is to leave him alone.*

If you'll just leave your name and address at the box office, we'll be glad to enroll your cat in the Golden Age Club. That's right, if your cat has reached the twilight years, it's about time you let him enjoy himself. Let him live a little, he has so little to live!

Perhaps the kindest thing you can do for your cat is to leave him alone. If he wants to sit in front of the refrigerator all day and snooze, let him! But, dear cat lovers, you must be conscientious about making a little adjustment in his dinner fare. There are a few simple culinary rules you can follow that will make the last few years of your cat's life a real pleasure.

The most important thing to remember is that your cat must get food that is nourishing as well as easy to digest. The older he gets, the harder it is for him to digest his food. Also, aging has its effect

*He should get smaller meals.*

on teeth, as well as stomach organs, arteries, and the like. So easily absorbed food is best. Make his meal finely chopped, and go back to the days of his youth and feed him strained baby foods!

Obviously, another important thing to remember about feeding your cat as he settles down in retirement is that he should get smaller meals. Any surplus weight your cat may put on because he's been eating like he did when he was young and active can be dangerous. After all, like with us humans, fat can accumulate around his heart, putting more of a strain on it and shortening his life considerably. So give him smaller meals.

And give him meals more frequently, even though they are smaller. This would give him great pleasure. He'd feel that no one had forgotten him in his declining years. And, in fact, no one should! There's another good reason for this. Some older cats have a tendency to vomit directly after eating. More frequent meals with less in them will help solve this problem.

*Your old cat is likely to have a finicky appetite as he gets older.*

If he does start to put on a little weight, the fact that you've cut down on the size of the meals and have fed him more frequently should compensate for his added weight.

Your old cat is likely to have a finicky appetite as he gets older. He may not exactly "leap" to his bowl when you blow chow call. How to get him interested in dinner? Simple. Appeal to his emotion. Just whomp up a hearty bowl of soup. There's less chewing involved for his sensitive teeth, and there's a high retention of nutrition. It's a strange old cat who doesn't fall for a delicious bowl of warm chicken soup!

Now you may think that you're just brimming over with the milk of human kindness when you give your old cat milk right out of the bottle, but actually you may be doing him harm! You see, the fat content of whole milk is too much for him now. So make it easy on him. Give him skim or powdered milk. Remember: the less fat, the less heart problem! There's no reason why he'd mind!

Here are a few hints in feeding your old cat: let him have a bone on occasion. Bones help preserve his teeth. Or you may want to go get a little chewy toy for him to play with—something that won't add any calories to his restricted diet. And, by the way, if you do get him a chew toy, don't get one made of the kind of rubber that he can bite off and swallow. This can make for really serious stomach problems!

If any foods disagree with him, eliminate them from his diet. After all, he's got a right to be choosy. He's lived long enough now to be entitled to *some* opinion about what he wants for dinner. Of course, if it's something which he *must* have, and he turns up his nose at it, make sure he gets it camouflaged in some clever way!

Vitamins and minerals are extremely important for old cats. They help him resist the inevitable geriatric diseases. Consult with your veterinarian about the proper vitamins and minerals to give him.

With these few simple rules in mind and the valuable information your veterinarian will be glad to provide, you can make your pet's last few years on earth quite peaceful and happy. After all, he deserves it!

*Vitamins and minerals are extremely important for old cats.*

## CHICKEN SOUP FOR CATS

*1 bouillon cube*
*½ cup water*
*Leftover chicken, boned*
*Grated cheese*

Dissolve bouillon cube in warm water. Cut up chicken into small pieces. Add bouillon to chicken, just enough to make soupy consistency. Sprinkle with grated cheese. Serve.

## YANGTZE BUBBLE

*1 strip bacon*
*½ can split-pea soup, undiluted*
*1 hard-cooked egg*
*Powdered milk*

Cook bacon, and drain grease so bacon is dry and crunchy. Warm soup. Cut up egg. Combine ingredients. Sprinkle with dry powdered milk. Serve.

## THE CAT'S WHISKERS

*¼ pound beef heart*
*Margarine*
*2 teaspoons cottage cheese*

Cut beef heart into small pieces. Sauté for 1 minute in margarine. Mix with cottage cheese. Serve.

## KIDNEY UNDER BLANKET

*¼ pound beef kidney*
*Margarine*
*2 strips bacon*
*Skim milk*

Cut up kidney into small picees. Sauté in margarine for 1 minute, turning frequently. Cook bacon. Pour some skim milk in bowl. Add kidney and top with cut-up bacon. Serve.

## CONTINENTAL DIVIDE*

> ¼ *pound beef heart*
> *Leftover carrots*
> ½ *small onion*
> ¼ *green pepper*
> *Margarine*

Cut heart into small pieces. Dice carrots, onion, and green pepper. Place all ingredients in frying pan with some margarine. Cook 2 minutes (or until heart turns brown). Serve warm.

## CHICKEN SUPERIOR

> ½ *cup leftover chicken*
> 1 *hard-cooked egg*
> 2 *tablespoons cat food*
> 1 *teaspoon cooking oil*

Cut chicken into small pieces. Cut and mash egg. Mix with cat food and cooking oil. Serve.

## MILKY WAY DELIGHT

To a handful of dry cat food add ½ cup skim milk and leftover meat chunks. Serve.

## TOAST 'N' ONION BLEND

> ½ *can baby onions*
> ½ *cup skim milk*
> 1 *slice toast*

Mash onions well in bowl. Add milk. Break up toast into small pieces and add to mixture. Serve.

## IMPROMPTU DINNER

¼ cup sour cream
Leftover fish
1 hard-cooked egg

Blend sour cream with mashed fish. Mash egg and mix. Serve.

## CHEESE AND BACON WHIP

2 slices bacon
2 tablespoons canned cat food
Grated cheese

Cook bacon and break up with fork. Mix with cat food. Sprinkle with grated cheese. Serve.

# 11

# Rewards and Special Treats

*There are times when you will want to feed your cat something special.*

When good old Uncle Bob's birthday comes up each year, or when Cousin Adelaide finally decides to get married, you probably send a gift. Naturally you feel so good about shopping for something special that you completely tear the hinges off your budget box. Well, you should. After all, it's a special occasion, and it deserves some special consideration.

The same holds true for your pet pet. There are times when you will want to feed your cat something special—give him a reward or special treat just to let him know that you love him just as much as he loves you. And why not? So here are some suggestions to help you when it comes time to cater to your cat.

When do you give your cat a special treat? His birthday is a festive occasion, and you may want to reward him then. Or, if you are going

*After grooming him is a good time for a reward.*

away on a trip and your cat is a little excited, you may want to reward him with a morsel *after* you arrive with him (if you give him anything just before traveling, he may be so excited that he won't be able to keep it down, or keep it in). After grooming him is a good time. Of course, if your cat is a new mother, you'll want to give her something special. And you may want to reward her kittens, too. When your kitten learns something new, like how to use his potty box (if he's an indoor cat), then reward him right after he uses it the first time. He's made you happy, and you should make him happy!

Every cat has his own favorite reward or special treat, but there are some that are known to be special favorites among the feline set.

Chicken innards make an especially fine treat. Either feed them raw (not cold, but at room temperature) or make a stew out of them with leftover vegetables. Include the liver, and your cat will flip. And speaking of liver, one friend favors rewarding her cats with chopped chicken liver on great occasions. Her cats sit and chew up the chicken liver as if they were in a Broadway delicatessen and had only ten minutes till the box office closed.

Eggs can make a very simple treat for your cat. The simplest and perhaps best way to reward your cat with an egg is by beating it up in a little milk and just serving it in his bowl. You may want to warm the milk and egg mixture, but it's not necessary. Although this is the same food you may feed your kitten, sometimes you should treat your adult cat as if he were a little kitty again. A variation of this treat is to add a little wheat germ to the milk and egg mixture.

Just as interesting, a special treat is the one that is served to an evil-looking black cat who belongs to a neighbor. This cat loves pancakes and syrup, while watching the kiddies' cartoons on television.

Of course you can go to the extreme in preparing special treats and rewards for your cat. But usually a simple delight is enough to satisfy your pet. A few crunchy cat biscuits (prepared for cats by the commercial pet food companies) or an egg, or even a little ice cream is enough.

And a word about ice cream and candy! Most cat owners agree

*The best reward, sometimes, is just to be left alone.*

*As long as you're up, get me a Grant's.*

that large quantities of ice cream and candy are not good for their cats. But on occasion a few licks of ice cream, or a little bit of candy (or those wonderful flapjacks and syrup) can be just the right reward for your cat.

The best reward your cat can get, sometimes, is just to be left alone. Of course, you'll want to do more than that, and rightly so! His favorite food will do the trick. So reach for the ice cream scoop while you're in the kitchen. Your cat deserves a special treat!

# 12
# Helpful Hints

*He must learn to live by your schedule.*

Here are some hints and short cuts you may find helpful toward planning meals for your cat:

1. You may want to feed your kitten an additional snack just before your own bedtime. (He may demand it!) You'll find that if you do, you won't be bothered by his wanting you to wake up in the middle of the night and start rattling pots and pans. A good bedtime snack will keep him filled up until morning.

2. Vary your cat's mealtime by an hour or so. This way he doesn't become used to a rigid schedule that you may not be able to follow. He must learn to live by *your* schedule if he's going to live in *your* house. After all, if you decide to sleep late this Sunday morning, you don't want to be awakened by a disturbed cat who tugs at your covers for his breakfast.

3. Don't let your cat leap to the dinner table for any reason! If he learns to roost on the table top, he'll soon learn that the table

is a sure spot for some sneaky stealing of your food. And there's no sense in allowing him to steal your food *before* you begin to eat it. Also, don't let him eat from your plate. He'll soon learn that he can get some of those luscious things he shouldn't have. Table scraps should be given to your cat at *your* discretion, not at his choosing. Always feed him in his own bowl, never out of your plate!

4. Cats can be sloppy eaters. (Some are—some aren't. Naturally *your* cat is the most fastidious diner since Emily Post!) Generally speaking, cats like to play with their food. So spread a newspaper (the book review section, preferably) under your cat's bowl. This will keep your floor and his food clean.

5. If you feed your cat canned food, and you must wear a clothespin on your nose while spooning it out into his bowl, try refrigerating the food, can and all. This will usually take away most of the smell. Also, the pet food companies make tight-fitting plastic tops that fit cans exactly. This helps keep the smell in the can rather than in your kitchen. But if you refrigerate your cat's dinner, don't serve it to him cold! Pour a little hot water over the entire meal before serving. This will warm it sufficiently for eating.

6. If your cat won't drink milk (and some cats won't) mix a little with his dinner. Or use powdered milk. Just mix with his meat.

*They like to play with their food.*

*If your cat won't eat, don't force him.*

The powder will be absorbed by both the food and the cat. Powdered milk is especially good for old cats and for summertime feeding, since it is low in fat content.

7. No matter how many cats you have, each one should have his own food bowl. Avoid feeding meals out of a "community" bowl, since the cats who are more polite (or less aggressive) will not get their fair share.

8. Believe it or not, your cat's appetite is not constant. Although sometimes you think that you have a pet who is all mouth and stomach, there are times when the most ravenous gluttons will go several days without eating. Don't worry. If your cat won't eat, don't force him. And don't try to coax him back to his bowl by tempting him with delicacies. You'll just spoil him. Take his food away from him after about fifteen minutes. Don't feed him again until his next regularly scheduled meal. If he doesn't eat yet, continue taking the plate away. Eventually he'll get hungry. He'll start eating again *when he's hungry!* Remember: cats don't live by clocks and watches as we do, so it's never *dinnertime,* except when prompted by a gnawing stomach. The thing to be particularly careful of when your cat does refuse his meals for a few days is that he's not ill. If there is something wrong with him, usually his symptoms show up in other ways too, and you'll know to go to your veterinarian.

9. Some cats like to eat alone, some with people around. After observing your cat for a few meals you'll find out which he prefers.

The interesting thing is that very few cats will eat when there's a stranger in the house.

10. A grinder or blender is a valuable asset. When you grind food for your cat, incorporate it all into one mixture. Cats are very clever. They try to separate the foods they like from the foods they dislike. And they usually do a pretty good job! So make sure you grind it up fine!

11. If your cat is a reluctant eater, you can feed him small bits and pieces of his dinner with your fingers. Of course, this is only to be done occasionally! Don't let him get into the habit! Another way to feed a reluctant cat is by pushing his dinner into a fresh mound. He may have tamped it down to the bottom of the bowl with his nose while eating so that he's unable to eat the remainder with ease. On the other hand, the most eager cats often eat the least. Your cat may come bounding up to his dinner, flailing the air with his sword and crying "Attack, attack!" only to become completely disinterested after the first few slurps. There's nothing wrong with him. He just has eyes bigger than his stomach!

12. Usually avoid giving bones to cats—especially fish bones and chicken bones. They'll splinter and stab your pet right where it hurts! If you do give him a bone, give him one from roast beef or veal. The bone is helpful to the kitten for calcium, and to the mature and old cat for tooth and gum exercise. Of course some pet owners disagree violently and won't allow their pets near bones. It's really up to you to decide. Naturally, you can ask your friendly veterinarian, and perhaps he'll be helpful in making your decision.

13. If your cat has a tendency to vomit, but is not sick, feed him small amounts of food a number of times a day. Probably his stomach can't take large amounts and this upsets him.

14. Occasionally (maybe once a week) give your cat a little oil. No, it doesn't help him eliminate his waste, but it does help prevent him from gathering a hairball in his stomach. What kind of oil

for cats? A little cod-liver oil or mineral oil or cooking oil. The most effective way to give your cat oil is to give it to him straight. Mixing it with his food negates its effectiveness. You may want to do this: open a can of sardines, eat the sardines for your own dinner and let your cat lick the oil that is left in the can. If your cat refuses oil of any kind, one way to make him take it is to rub it on his feet. In the normal course of events, he'll lick it off, satisfying his desire for outer cleanliness and your desire for his inner cleanliness.

15. If you have a fat cat, you can melt away those extra pounds two ways. (a) Reduce the amount of food your cat eats. He may come away from the bowl scratching for more food, but don't give it to him. He'll eventually get used to eating less. Your veterinarian can be a great help in advising you about meal planning. (b) Make sure your cat gets more exercise. Play ball with him. Make hanging toys for him just out of reach, so that he must stretch to get them. Use any method to make him more active.

16. If you plan to travel with your cat, don't feed him for four to five hours previous to your departure. Cats get nervous and anxious before great events like trips, and they could easily get an upset stomach. When you do arrive at your destination, cats are almost always constipated for a while, until they get used to their new surroundings. If you do take along food for your cat, make sure it's the kind of·food he's used to eating. Take dry food, since it won't spoil. And take water. Some people like to take a jar of water from home, since different localities have different-tasting water and their pet may object to "foreign" water.

You will find many hints and short cuts of your own which are a great help in your culinary escapades. Each cat is different, and thus the short cuts one person finds applicable may not suit another. The few hints mentioned above are somewhat universal, though not the final word on calculated cooking for your cat. You will probably find more in your own searches. So keep on searching!

*The End*